A Woman's Voice

~ Inspirational Short Stories ~

Volume 2

DOLORES AYOTTE

A Woman's Voice (Inspirational Short Stories) Volume 2
Copyright © 2014 by Dolores Ayotte. All rights reserved.

No part of this publication may be reproduced, stored in a retrieval system or transmitted in any way by any means, electronic, mechanical, photocopy, recording or otherwise without the prior permission of the author except as provided by Canada and United States copyright law.

Book design copyright © 2014 by Dolores Ayotte. All rights reserved.
Cover design by Dolores Ayotte
Interior design by Dolores Ayotte
Printed by CreateSpace
Published in Canada
ISBN: 978-0-9948673-2-2
Self-Help, Motivational & Inspirational

Disclaimer: The suggestions provided in this inspirational book are based on a personal point of view and not in any professional capacity.

The Human & Humane Self-Help Author

Dolores holds a Bachelor of Arts degree with a major in psychology from the University of Winnipeg as well as teacher certification from the University of Manitoba. She has also taken courses in human relationships and communication.

Her self-help books are written in retrospect based on a proven recipe, one she has incorporated step by step into her own life. Over time, Dolores eventually developed better life coping skills which inspired her to put pen to paper and write four previous books about her experiences. She utilizes quotes, anecdotes, humor, and her own personal stories when necessary to make her suggestions relevant and to give an example of how to use her simple tips in daily living.

She is now retired and spends half the year with her husband at a retirement community in Arizona. For the remainder of the year, Dolores enjoys her children and grandchildren in Winnipeg, Manitoba where she was born and raised. She continues to learn from all the people who touch her life.

Table of Contents

Introduction

1   The Inception of A Woman's Voice

2   The Feminine Spirit

3   Me, Myself, and I

4   The Coupon Queens

5   Storytelling

6   Pointing the Way

7   Embracing the Power Within

8   Reconciliation versus Resolution

9   LAFF (until your stomach aches)

10   The Stigma of Mental Illness

11   Underdogs

12   Dealing with Depression

13   Life's Journey

14   Dealing with Anger

15   Dreams

16   Childless Mother

17   Having a Bad Day

18   Forgiveness

19   Added Talent

Conclusion

Bonus Chapter - *A Woman's Voice Volume 1 ~ The Empty Nest*

Bonus Chapters - *Growing Up and Liking It ~*
Introduction and Shake It Off

Introduction

"Writing makes a person very vulnerable. It opens you to public criticism, to ridicule, to rejection. But it also opens conversation and thought. It stirs minds, and touches hearts. It brings us into contact with our souls. So how can it possibly be a waste of time, an idle act, a mistake, a betrayal of truth? Who can possibly tell us not to do it?" ~ Joan Chittister, Order of Saint Benedict

This quote really hits home for me. How many of us feel discouraged by the lack of response we get to what we write? How many of us have felt vulnerable by what we have written and how people might view us? How many of us have been ridiculed, perhaps even mocked, criticized, or rejected because of what we have shared? How many of us have had what we thought were friends and then they used what we have written to hurt us. Sharing our heart is similar to wearing our hearts on our sleeves…it leaves us wide open. As writers, we truly become open books. So why do we do it? I have the answer in a nutshell, at least from my point of reference. There is a niggling inside of us that just won't go away until we put pen to paper and write our thoughts. There is a deep thirst inside an author that will only be quenched by having or making the opportunity to express these inner seeds that start off so small but manage to become a book one day.

I know that I have felt several of the previously mentioned emotions. I have also known disappointment and discouragement but…I totally agree with this quote by Joan Chittister. My writing has stoked conversations outside of people's natural comfort zones. People have opened up to me and told me about their personal struggles because they know I understand and have compassion for their plight. My words have also stirred minds and touched hearts as I spur on people to think for themselves. I also encourage others to learn to love themselves in order to truly love, accept, and respect others. Believe me, this is no easy feat and not one I take lightly.

Writing is no "idle act", no "mistake", and not meant to be "a betrayal of truth". At least, not my writing anyway. Writing is a gift that has been bestowed upon me and many others like me who want to share their talent with the world. To do less or to bury this talent would be a betrayal, not only to myself but to my Maker, the One who so generously and abundantly gives us all a variety of gifts to share with our fellow humankind. Yes…sometimes it can hurt, but the rewards for our desire to share this wondrous gift usually far outweigh the negative consequences. Therefore, I salute all my fellow writers today. Chin up. Even if we positively touch only a few people with our written words, we have touched a whole world to God. I also salute those who take or make the time to read our words. Without them...we would be like a tree that falls in the forest with no one around to hear the sound of its impact. Yes indeed...as an author I have something to say. If you are an author reading my words, you know exactly what I mean. If you are a reader of inspirational books, you are honoring me beyond words by reading what is near and dear to my heart. Hopefully, what I have to share will touch your heart in a very intimate way.

You are about to read A Woman's Voice ~ Volume 2. In the first chapter I will give you a little preamble as to its inception. It will better explain why this inspirational book has been written and what you can expect if you decide to read on. At the end of most chapters, there will be a series of motivational questions. You, as the reader can opt to write down the answers or you can choose to mentally reflect upon them...either way, the key is to be honest with yourself. Personal reflection can be seen as a gentle reminder that as life goes on we have many opportunities to live, learn, and reflect on life in general. We also have every opportunity to learn from these reflections to help ensure that history doesn't repeat itself. One of my daughters recently made a poignant observation on life. She states that if we don't learn our lessons the first time around, opportunities to get it straight will keep arising until we do. Makes perfect sense to me. How many times do we get into the same kind of fix and we ask ourselves "why" we are facing these same perplexing situations over and over again. Well...in my opinion, I think my daughter has effectively answered this question. We didn't learn our lesson the first time around.

In order to add some levity to this inspirational book, I have interspersed some lighter topics in between the more serious ones. All work and no play is not nearly as much fun as a combination of them both. Wouldn't you agree?

As usual, I have utilized numerous quotes and anecdotes from both women and men alike in order to add to your reading pleasure. I prefer to draw from a wide wealth of wisdom and enjoy the sagacity of both genders. I also recommend that you read all of my books in doses, not unlike taking medicine. These motivational writings are not meant to be read in one or two sittings like fictional books and perhaps other non-fictional books. My books are meant to be digested in small doses in order to reflect upon and perhaps glean the guidance that we may need to develop skills to better cope with the challenges of life.

1 ~ The Inception of A Woman's Voice

"Remember no one can make you feel inferior without your consent." ~ Eleanor Roosevelt

I recently had a lovely conversation with one of my twin daughters. A few years ago, she had the wonderful occasion to attend a conference in Los Angeles, California. I could clearly hear the enthusiasm and pleasure in her voice as she described her experience to me. This was a conference for women and by women. Attendees varied in ages from, twenty-something, to a woman in her eighties. They all had a common goal…they wanted to find their voices and learn to better express themselves. In other words, they all desired the same end goal. These women wanted to be "heard".

Before I share a small part of her experience with you, I want to relate to you how she heard about this special event in the first place. My daughter is a social worker who has been a stay-at-home mother for the last several years. She has had four children in a ten year span and they keep her challenged and extremely busy. She has chosen to put her career on hold in order to meet the ever growing demands of her little family.

Before this particular conference, her husband sent her the information via e-mail giving her the heads up about this event specifically geared for women knowing that it would be of great interest to her. I chuckled to myself when my daughter told me she emailed her husband back at work to ask him "why" he would send this information to her when he knew full well that she would be unable to attend due to her busy home life and domestic demands. Guess what happened next? Her husband must have secretly wanted her to go because he helped make it happen. He took on the responsibilities of their young family for almost five days so that my daughter could benefit from this learning opportunity. She was about to experience a first time adventure by getting away alone to enjoy a totally new and exciting experience.

The presenter of this conference was speaking on a particular topic (women's voices) for the first time. Therefore, my daughter was part of the inception stage of this relevant topic by the organizer of the conference. Approximately five hundred women from all over Canada and the United States attended. In a nutshell, the theme of the conference was about the voices of women and the desire to be heard. My daughter was given this great opportunity because her husband made the choice to instinctively hear her voice and helped create the occasion for her to meet with other women in their efforts to also be heard.

In my opinion, my daughter actually already had a voice at home because her husband was instrumental in getting her to the conference. It was apparent to me that no matter what our walk in life may be, we can have the opportunity to have a voice. In other words, that voice starts in the home. Once it is heard there it can evolve into other forums as well.

Shortly thereafter, my daughter returned home a much more enlightened and contented individual. The fire was burning strong inside her with the keen desire to make a difference in this, oftentimes, troubled world we call home. Her enthusiasm lit my fire too. Yes…we all have a voice and we all want to be heard. Now, the real challenge is yet to unfold as we make every effort to find someone who is willing to listen. We often hear the expression that someone is "a gifted speaker". I have a sneaking suspicion that the seldom…if ever used expression…"a gifted listener", is nearly common as "a gifted speaker" or viewed as equally important.

Trust me…it is.

"Don't compromise yourself. You are all you've got." ~ Betty Ford

"If better is possible, good is not enough." ~ Source Unknown

Personal Reflections:

1. Do you consider yourself to have a voice in either the work place or at home?
2. If so, are you communicating effectively and truly expressing yourself as an equal when you have the opportunity to speak?
3. Do you have the tendency to voice your opinion only when it agrees with strong-minded individuals or do you feel strong enough with your own voice and personal views to publicly disagree with others? Hint: A good example of not feeling comfortable with your views is having the tendency to discuss them afterwards with a friend or co-worker whom you know will agree with you and your take on things.

2 ~ The Feminine Spirit ~ Andrea Ayotte Cockerill

"A strong woman knows she has strength enough for the journey, but a woman of strength knows it is in the journey where she will become strong." ~ Source Unknown

A woman's voice...

What does she sound like? She is fierce, intuitive, and powerful, for she is aware of her own relevance. Her knowledge runs deep, fueled with the passion coming from the women that have come before her. She looks into the eyes of the little ones around her knowing that if she denies her worth, she denies the worth of the next generation of femininity to come.

She has experienced the deep personal pain of having ignored the whispers of her own soul, or when she has had the courage to speak up and then quickly backing down yet again. She sees the women around her struggling as well, many overeating to try to temper the power within.

Others may spend too much money or try to portray perfection, or they may devalue the role they play in the lives of their families and communities. Just maybe if these women could keep their minds busy enough, they won't see where they have either given up their voices or where they have been taken from them.

At last, she knows the courage it will take to speak her truth as she can no longer sacrifice her spirit. When she felt that her voice was irrelevant, she cared that others did not hear her. Now she feels her relevance deep within her soul and no longer seeks out the confirmation that it is worth something…that she is worth something. There is a deep freedom in honoring and celebrating the fierceness that resides in the inner voice of a woman.

It is this power that if collectively used, will create deep and everlasting changes for the world we live in and for the generations to follow. She thanks the women before her, who have used their strength and wisdom to make it easier for her, and she uses the next generation as an inspiration to continue to find the courage to stand tall.

"You have to accept whatever comes and the only important thing is that you meet it with courage and with the best you have to give." ~ Eleanor Roosevelt

"We are what we repeatedly do. Excellence, then, is not an act but a habit." ~ Source Unknown

Note: The previous article was written by my daughter who I mentioned in The Inception of A Woman's Voice, the first chapter of this inspirational book. The questions I am about to add are my own.

Personal Reflections:
1. Is your voice fierce and intuitive or shy and reserved?
2. Do you feel that you have a powerful position in life whereby you can influence others and feel good about it?
3. Do you consider yourself to be a positive person?
4. Are you comfortable in your own skin?

3 ~ Me, Myself, and I

"There is an infinite difference between a little wrong and just right, between fairly good and the best, between mediocrity and superiority..." ~ *Orison Swett Marden*

I have a nickname given to me by my husband. It is Bob. Many years ago, one of my grandchildren started calling me Bob. She was learning how to talk and for whatever reason, when she saw me, the name Bob popped out of her mouth. Perhaps she was trying to call me Baba and it lovingly came out as Bob. Over the years, my husband has formed the habit of teasing me and calling me by that very name. I don't mind at all as it brings back such fond memories of a very precious time in my life.

It has been my observation that at times in life, it is very easy to dwell on ourselves and not look around at the people in our lives and what they are up to or what they stand for in terms of their beliefs. Many times over the years my husband and I have come to use the expression it's "all about Bob" to describe when either one of us becomes too self-focused or self-absorbed. We also tend to say this when we notice that we have lost some of our objectivity. It is very difficult to not fall into the trap of being very interested in what's going on in our own lives and not interested enough in what's going on the lives of those around us. We've observed that we are not alone in the ability to engage in this not-so-attractive behavior.

Personally, one of my pet peeves in life is to be in a relationship that is one-sided and off balance. I neither want to offer this to my friends nor do I expect to receive it from them. If we become "all about Bob" people or if we hang out with "all about Bob" people we soon become disenchanted with the friendship. My goal in life is to strive for balanced relationships where we are both interested in what is going on in each other's life.

I must admit that I no more want it to be all about someone else than I want it to be all about me. Relationships are about relating to each other. It's not about some lopsided pseudo friendship whereby one gets to talk and the other gets to listen most or all of the time. What fun is that? In my opinion, this kind of relationship won't stand the test of time because if it's too one-sided and eventually one or the other will get emotionally tapped out or just plain frustrated with the lack of reciprocity.

I realize that there may be times in a person's life when they may need a compassionate ear or require more support;

however, if it is usually this way even during the good times, the relationship is doomed to fail from the onset. We all have needs and they must be fulfilled in varying degrees in order for a true and long lasting friendship to unfold. I have no desire for people to look at me and think I am an "all about Bob" personality. However, I can honestly say that I don't want to always be in the audience either or what I have come to refer to as someone else's personal fan club.

I want a healthy balance when it comes to the friendships in my life. I have no desire to play "show and tell" and not take a turn. I already did that when I was an elementary school teacher. It may not be necessary for it to be fifty-fifty all of the time, but as previously stated, there does have to be some reciprocity in order to feel validated in any long term quality relationship.

Once again I stress that I have no desire for it to be all about me, myself, and I, but on the other hand the reverse also holds true. I don't want it to be all about you, yourself, and yours each and every time we get together. In my opinion, it is no better to be always "giving" than it is to be always "taking" in any relationship. There has to be a happy medium in order to feel satisfied.

Life is a matter of give and take and this concept works best for most people.

"Yesterday is a cancelled check; tomorrow is a promissory note; today is the only cash you have so spend it wisely." ~ Kay Lyons

Personal Reflections:

1. When you are sharing a conversation or communicating with a friend, do you do more than your fair share of talking or do you listen more?
2. Would you consider it to be a balanced relationship? If not, is it what you really want or are you settling for less in order to not ruffle any feathers and keep the status quo?
3. Is it okay to want balance and equality in your friendships? Do you feel more fulfilled in this type of relationship?

4 ~ The Coupon Queens

"People seldom improve when they have no other model but themselves to copy after." ~ Goldsmith

It seems so much easier to admit some of our silly, little habits when we find people who operate much the same way. My mom was one of the biggest coupon people I know. She loved cutting out coupons and taking them to the store to redeem them for cash. The stores weren't nearly so sticky all those years ago and they would dole out cash for your coupons whether you bought the product or not. My mom loved this little practice because money was tight in those days and this coupon money ended up being her extra cash to spend the way she saw fit.

I'm a coupon clipper. There's no getting around this fact. The other day when I went to the local pharmacy with my wallet full of coupons, I got a bunch of excellent deals. When I jumped into the car and looked in the mirror, I realized I had become my mother. Oh my, I could hardly believe it. I not only look like her, I'm now doing the same darn thing. The scary part about it is that the realization crept up on me in such an unexpected way that it brought a smile to my face.

I don't really need to engage in this habit. I'm not in the same position my mom was all those years ago, so why do I do it? I'll tell you why. I have a group of friends that I socialize with and guess what? We all do the exact same thing. It's actually hilarious. It's a wonderful game that we all seem to enjoy. We go shopping and to restaurants with our handy coupons. Buy one meal, get one free has been the deciding factor in many of the restaurants we frequent. There is even a half-price day at the local movie theater. Our husbands have started to be as hooked as we are and they are cooperating to the fullest extent. Usually you can only purchase one item per coupon, so the guys sometimes join us so that they can use a coupon too. You know how much these men like to go shopping but yet somehow or other we get them to come along with us so we can benefit from two coupons instead of just one.

As I'm writing this and trying to describe this habit of ours, it makes me want to burst out laughing. Here we are…all excelling in the art of being thrifty. We are so proud of our bargains. When we're gone and leave our children their inheritance, if there's any to be had, I'm sure they'll spend it faster than you can "shake a stick" and probably without a moment's hesitation. We've had a blast saving our money. Hopefully, our children will have as big a blast spending it. What do you think?

"Every job is a self-portrait of the person who did it. Autograph your work with excellence." ~ Source Unknown

Personal Reflections:

1. Do you have any quirky little habits?
2. Do you see how we form some of these habits based on past experience or from those who have influenced us in some of our past decisions?
3. Do you ever look in the mirror and can hardly believe who you are and what you've become?
4. Every experience is a learning opportunity…try not to forget that your children and grandchildren are observing a lot more that you might think. What kind of an example are you setting for them?

5 ~ Storytelling

"To live is so startling it leaves little time for anything else." ~ Emily Dickinson

It brings me great pleasure to elaborate on my philosophy of my love for storytelling and the motivation behind the desire to share my humor, my true life experiences, and my innermost self. I delight in sharing the stories of others as well, in order to better get my points across or to enhance the lives of those who want to vicariously benefit by listening and learning from those who have gone before them.

Our telling one another's stories can be a means of extending not only their reach in touching other people's lives, but our own hand as we reach out to help others attain their full potential as followers of Christ. As a result, we are in the process of learning to strive together to attain our true aspirations and capabilities as human beings. In doing so, we help each other achieve this desired common goal to become the "Body" of Christ on earth.

In helping others, we ourselves, are being helped. The mutuality of the relationship forms the foundation of all that we are as Christians. When we grasp each other's hand in this way, we form a circle of God's love and create the chain of His Divine Essence as we link up with like-minded individuals.

It is the combination of reaching out and reaching back that binds us together in the most profound way. It is the fabric that knits us together as humankind.

"You may not be responsible for your heritage, but you are responsible for your future." ~ Source Unknown

Inspirational poem
"No vision and you perish; No ideal and you're lost;
Your heart must ever cherish some faith at any cost.
Some hope, some dream to cling to, some rainbow in the sky,
Some melody to sing to, some service that is high."
~ Harriet Du Autermont

Personal Reflections:

1. Do you find that you understand a concept better if an example or a story is used to better explain it?
2. When a story is shared with you, can you or do you mentally relate to it at times?

3. Do you find comfort in knowing that similar situations have occurred in your own life?
4. Is there comfort in knowing you are not alone?
5. When people listen to your stories or life experiences, does it bring you comfort when they can relate to your situation?

6 ~ Pointing the Way

"To succeed is nothing-it's an accident. But to feel no doubts about oneself is something very different: it is character." ~ *Marie Leneru*

At times, I know that I have a somewhat different philosophy on life than other individuals. I have always considered myself to be a teacher even before I had formal credentials. Although I left the classroom many years ago, the classroom has never left me. I feel like I am now very much "a teacher without walls". When I did teach elementary school, we used to have "show & tell" on a regular basis. The children loved this little practice, as I am sure they still do to this day in many classrooms around the world.

I think the children enjoyed when another child had a story to tell but I think they especially enjoyed when they had something to show. This visual aid made their story all the more enjoyable. As teachers, we also had a little saying that goes something like this. Tell me and I forget…Show me and I remember…Involve me and I learn. It has been my experience that telling someone what we think or believe may not always leave the mark we want it to. Showing them by leading with our example may have a greater impact and others will probably get a better idea of our message. Involving these individuals in what we are trying to teach will indeed have the greatest effect.

One of the things I have come to realize is that when we involve others, it is also necessary to know when to get out-of-the-way so that they can see the path clearly ahead. A good teacher needs to know when to "back off" and let the student forge ahead on their own. If we are constantly pointing the way, we could very well be hampering the student's line of vision and future learning experiences. Therefore, at some point, we may actually be doing them more harm than good.

Part of being more than a good teacher is knowing when to stop teaching and "let go…let God". The time when good teachers become great ones is when we figure this out. Do you know when to "back off" when necessary or "teach" when needed? It is no easy feat to discern. Therefore, being the most effective teacher may be a task similar to doing a balancing act or walking a tight rope. It's a slippery slope to say the least.

There is also a very fine line between what is seen as preaching versus teaching. Preaching may have a negative connotation if it isn't done in the right setting. We must be in tune, not only with ourselves but with those around us, in order to achieve the best results. Effective teaching usually has a way of positively involving others. I'm not so sure that preaching is seen in this same light. Preaching by our peers can be seen as a lot about telling and very little about showing or involving. Being told what to do or how to behave doesn't always achieve the desired positive results. We all have the opportunity to teach or to preach in our everyday lives. What I'm suggesting, is that we take a moment and ask ourselves how we're coming across.

"For every failure, there's an alternative course of action. You just have to find it. When you come to a roadblock, take a detour." ~ Mary Kay Ash

"Life is my college." ~ Louisa May Alcott

Personal Reflections:

1. Do you agree that there is a difference between teaching and preaching?
2. Would you agree that a sermon at church would be considered preaching?
3. When a friend/family member is sharing their experiences with you for your benefit in order to

help you better cope with your possible problems, would you consider this to be a form of teaching?

4. Do you agree that both teaching and preaching can be beneficial but they each have their place?

5. Would you agree that both teaching and preaching must be handled very carefully in order to not "talk down" to others? In my opinion, relating to others by sharing our similar experiences and how we coped helps even out the playing field. What are your thoughts on this?

7 ~ Embracing the Power Within
Andrea Ayotte Cockerill

"I am only one; but still I am one. I cannot do everything, but still I can do something; I will not refuse to do the something I can do." ~ Helen Keller

The other day I had an epiphany but it wasn't the kind of epiphany that makes one feel great and connected to God. It was the kind of awakening that actually brought me great sadness for its truth could not be denied. In many ways I have tried to feed a hunger inside myself with things that could never fill the gnawing feeling this hunger created. I have tried many times to search deep within, looking for answers that may comfort its emptiness. Maybe if I could fit in on the outside by measuring up to societies outward markers, I wouldn't feel so lonely on the inside.

I have come to understand, with great sadness, that at some level my loneliness comes from my own hunger of wanting to belong yet feeling like somehow I have fallen short of this goal. I had previously concluded that if I was special in some outwardly way then maybe that elusive gift of feeling this sense of belonging would be within my grasp.

What a painful feeling it is to feel like there is nothing particularly special about who you are, just because you are you.

My instinct is to distract myself from such uncomfortable sadness but by learning to run and face its shadow, the power it holds lessens. As its power lessens, my own sense of who I am increases which is something I am no longer willing to sacrifice. I have decided to stand in this shadow of distorted thinking and embrace its lessons. Soon I will be able to see that my specialness is derived from just being created in the image of God and that nothing else on my part needs to be done to gain the sense of belonging that I desire.

May you too find your own courage to look deep within to claim your own power and to celebrate your specialness that's always been there simply because you were created with love.

Inspirational Poem
   As I stretch towards the center of you,
   in silence I find the space that exists between the mind and the heart,
   and I am reminded that there is nothing to fear.
   Nothing can separate me from this place of comfort.

But in order to reach it,

I must pass through a moment that lies just between letting go

and the moment I grab hold of you.

It is my faith that bridges this divide.

When I reach you it becomes clear.

All I was ever meant to do, forever and for always, was to love myself.

All I was every meant to do, forever and for always, was to love you.

~ *Andrea Cockerill*

"He who loses wealth loses much; he who loses a friend loses more; but he that loses courage loses all."
~ *Cervantes*

Note: Once again this article was written by my daughter who I mentioned in the first chapter of this inspirational book. The chapter referred to is titled The Inception of A Woman's Voice. The questions I am about to add are my own.

Personal Reflections:

1. Do you ever feel lonely?

2. Do you sometimes even feel lonely when surrounded by people? In other words, is it possible to feel alone in a crowd?
3. What do you do to overcome these feelings?
4. Do you consider yourself to be special? If so…why? If not…why not?
5. Do you have a difficult time seeing your self-worth? If so…re-read the previous poem. Hint: Learning to love yourself as you are is one of the keys.

8 ~ Reconciliation versus Resolution

"The cure for all the ills and wrongs, the cares, the sorrows, and the crimes of humanity, all lie in the one word 'love'. It is the divine vitality that everywhere produces and restores life." ~ Lydia Maria Child

A while back I read an article that mentioned the difficulties a family had experienced before and after the death of their mother. The author of this article went on to say that she prayed for things to be resolved amongst her siblings and herself. The answer from God wasn't quite what she expected but regardless of this fact, in the end she felt that her prayers were answered nonetheless. Reading this article motivated me to have a look at my own life and my personal ideas about resolution and reconciliation. Is there a difference between the two concepts and if so what is it? Before further discussing this topic, I decided that the best course of action was to look up the exact meaning of these two words in the dictionary.

One definition for the word resolution that I found in a well-known dictionary is *"the power to make choices and set goals and to act upon them firmly in spite of opposition or difficulty"*. Another definition is *"unwavering firmness of character or action"*. Yet another is *"the quality of mind enabling one to face danger or hardship resolutely"*. When I look at one of the meanings to the word resolution I interpret it to be a strong belief or take on a certain situation that others may not agree with. More than likely the resolute person recognizes this fact and will act on their convictions regardless of the opposing view. I think that once we are resolute in our position, we may become unwavering no matter the consequences. One of these consequences may very well be choosing to stand alone. To me, the key words are *"to make choices and set goals and to act upon them firmly in spite of opposition or difficulty"*. In deciding this course of action, we become resolute in our beliefs and actions regardless of the outcome. It is truly having such a strong belief in our own convictions that we are prepared to, not only stand behind them, but also to stand alone in acting on them.

When I looked up the word reconciliation in the same dictionary, I discovered that there were also several definitions. The meaning that stuck out the most was *"to bring something into a state of agreement or accord"*. After careful consideration, I would have to say that reconciliation/agreement is not always attainable in every conflicting situation. Perhaps, the initial noble goal in any disagreement is to try to achieve a reconciliation whenever possible but if an agreement cannot be reached, then the next step is to try to zero in on a compromise in order to resolve the situation. However, if this option doesn't pan out, a responsible resolution to any given problem may very well be to choose the concept of "agreeing to disagree" in a respectful way. In reality, neither party is prepared to bend. I think that the writer of the previously mentioned article was alluding to this fact with her family. Obviously, they were not going to agree, but no one was willing to compromise on their stand. In other words, it was a stalemate. However, by "agreeing to disagree" in a loving way, they resolved their problematic family situation to her satisfaction. Therefore, God did answer her prayers and she was grateful for this fact.

In truth, this woman admits that she had been praying for reconciliation with her family in the hope that they would all agree. This did not happen. In the end they resolved the situation by rising above their differences; albeit, this was not her first choice. However, the only possible answer to her prayers obviously was what unfolded between the family members. This type of resolution means being open-mined enough to accept that reconciliation is not possible for the parties concerned. The best course of action is to just accept this fact and move on with life in a respectful and civil way. Resolution does not change anyone's stand. Resolution at its best, is the sincere and meaningful decision or act of "agreeing to disagree" without rancor. In my opinion, if there is still rancor, the issue is not really resolved. It is merely beneath the surface waiting for another occasion to rear its ugly head. It takes much courage to face such disagreements head on and to deal with them intelligently, maturely, and without any negative residual consequences. This goal is no easy feat to be sure.

"Choice, not chance, determines destiny." ~ Source Unknown

"The scar that you acquire by exercising courage will never make you feel inferior." ~ D.A. Battista

Personal Reflections:
1. Do you believe in the term irreconcilable differences? Personally…I do.
2. If you do too and you realize that you are never going to agree on a certain point of view or way of

acting, do you try to deal with it head on or do you try to avoid confrontation?

3. If you face the problem head on and come to the conclusion that you have arrived at a stalemate and you are never going to agree, what would you consider to be a reasonable course of action?

4. For me…not all disagreements are deal breakers, what about you? What I am basically saying is that some areas of disagreement are more serious than others. In other words, some can be overlooked depending on the situation and others cannot. It is up to the individuals involved to make that decision.

9 ~ LAFF (until your stomach aches)

Do you enjoy doing any kind of puzzle fun like Crosswords, Four Squares, Cryptograms, etc.? I personally engage in solving a variety of puzzles and word games including Jigsaw Puzzles, Word scraper, Scrabble...I love them all!

I am fascinated by the English language and how rule oriented it is on one hand and totally not on the other. We all know how phonics works and how you can sound out words. Sometimes it is as easy as pie and other times it doesn't make one ounce of sense because there are so many exceptions to the rules.

One such word that catches my attention is the word LAUGH. Why isn't it just spelled like it sounds...LAFF? Do you want to know why I much prefer this version?

At times when I struggle in my relationships with other people, I spell it this way. It's kind of like an anagram for me and perhaps you can use it as one for yourself too as you have a closer look at life.

L - Love

A – Accept

F – Forgive

F – Forget

When someone has either purposely or unintentionally offended me, if I learn to LAFF, then I can genuinely LAUGH it off and better enjoy my life. A well-developed sense of humor can really enhance life. You may have to work at it, but it is well worth the effort. LAFFTER really is the best medicine!

Personal Reflections:

1. Have you really learned to LAFF in life? Do you know that until we engage in this form of LAFFTER at the deepest level, it is very difficult to achieve inner peace and contentment?

2. Do you know that in order to truly LAFF with others, it is necessary to learn to LAFF with ourselves first? In other words, we must love and accept who we are and then learn from and forgive ourselves for our past mistakes. If we learn to "not be" so hard on ourselves by recognizing our own human frailties, we will be more compassionate and understanding toward others. Last but not least, it is wise to forgive and forget the offensive behavior;

however, try your best to not forget the lesson learned otherwise history may repeat itself.
3. Have you honed your sense of humor? Do you take things too seriously? Once again I repeat, have you learned to LAFF at yourself?

10 ~ The Stigma of Mental Illness

Memories are the key not to the past, but to the future. I know that the experiences of our lives, when we let God use them, become the mysterious and perfect preparation for the work He will give us to do." ~ Corrie Ten Boom

Over the last several years I have had the opportunity through my writing and publishing of books to personally share my efforts to deal with depression and other forms of mental illness. I was prompted to write my inspirational books for basically two reasons. I am a depression survivor. I know the despair and debilitating effects of major depression. The reason I refer to myself as a survivor means I have figured out ways to effectively deal with overcoming my depression. It took not only months, but years, of dogged determination to move past this illness. Even despite my success, I still have to face the cyclical periods it poses and deal with this illness when it creeps up.

I am grateful to say that I have lived a full and rewarding life despite this baffling condition. I consider myself to be very fortunate because the initial prognosis by the medical professionals was not very optimistic. In my early thirties, I was told that I would be on medication for the rest of my life. I flatly refused to accept this course of action. I have worked long and hard to come up with better life coping skills and I have succeeded. It's not to say that I never get depressed, it's only to say that I am better able to handle the situation when I do.

The other reason I am writing this chapter is that it coincides with the above quote. My experience with depression has enabled me to *"become the mysterious and perfect preparation for the work"* God has planned for me. I feel that I am being called upon to be an advocate to share my experiences so that others will be encouraged to speak more freely about theirs. In this way, perhaps the "stigma" attached to mental illness will continue to decline. My heart has gone out to people who have shared some of their stories with me. As a result, I would like to share some of these stories with you. Dealing with mental illness is never easy whether you are the person suffering with the symptoms or the family members and friends supporting the mentally ill individual. This heart wrenching story explains more.

One anonymous acquaintance says… *"After more than 14 years of symptoms, I finally couldn't let my mother go untreated anymore. We had been trying to get her to go for voluntary treatment for years. I had her committed against her will and after a 6 month stay in a mental facility she is now staying with my brother who makes sure she takes her medication. She was diagnosed with Schizophrenia, but because it took so long for treatment to start, she will never be the same person she was. She lives in her own world now and is unable to communicate in any significant way with people. I would love to see the perception of general public change towards Schizophrenia. Most people believe that it gives the person suffering from it split personalities and that they hear voices and that they are all homicidal. Truth is Schizophrenia is characterized with 'hallucinations' of all the senses, sight, hearing, touch, taste, but it also breaks down the person's ability to interact in social settings. My mother was smart enough to hide the worst of the symptoms from us for many years. If the 'acceptability' of mental illness was better, she might not have tried hiding it."*

Another anonymous acquaintance states… *"Undoubtedly there are many people who still bear a stigmatizing attitude towards mental illness, some of whom may even direct that towards certain sufferers they encounter. That is sad. However, I'm sure that there are many other people who do not have that negative attitude or mindset, and yet fail to encourage and show acts of kindness, because they don't understand the sufferer's needs. They don't want to offend, or are afraid that their words or attempts at kindness may offend and 'set (the individual) off,' and result in rejection. My wife and I have experienced this during our years of pastoral ministry. However, we learned through repeated exposure and experience to look and care beyond the episode of the moment."*

Personally, I think education and public awareness will eventually help individuals to show more compassion and empathy towards those with mental health issues. The care givers also need the support and encouragement of others because they are deeply affected as well.

"Expect trouble as an inevitable part of life and repeat to yourself the most comforting words of all: "This, too, shall pass." ~ Ann Landers

"The mind, like a parachute, functions only when open." ~ Source Unknown

Personal Reflections:

1. Do you or does anyone close to you suffer from any form of mental illness?
2. Is the illness out in the open in a similar way that one might be open about a physical illness?

3. If you are having an "off" day or dealing with bouts of depression, do you try to hide it from others? If so, why?
4. Do you feel there is a stigma to having a mental illness?

11 ~ Underdogs

Little minds are tamed and subdued by misfortune, but great minds rise above them." ~ Washington Clark

Have you ever considered yourself to be an underdog? Although I have internally referred to myself as an underdog many times, I'm not quite certain that I know exactly what this expression means. Instead of going into a big diatribe about what I think it means, I just want to use it in the sense that actually applies to me and my life. In past publications, I've already described that I had poor and simple roots as far as my background is concerned. My parents were not well-educated, although nor were many of their peers. I don't want to say that I was born on the wrong side of the tracks, but I'm sure there were some people who thought that's exactly where I lived in my youth.

I remember the mother of my closest childhood friend telling her daughter that she didn't want her to play with me. You know what little children are like, they repeat things verbatim. My friend, who was an only child, didn't hesitate to share this information with me. I came from a family of six children and we didn't live in the most desirable neighborhood. There was a single mother on welfare next door to us living with her nine children. There were other kids in the area who were always up to some kind of mischief. Some of the boys would get into pretty serious trouble and a few of them ended up in reform school for juvenile delinquents. Mind you, by today's standards with all that is going on with drugs and gangs etc., what these boys were up to is probably what the police would now consider to be "small potatoes". My dad was pretty strict with us as children but there is no way that he could have prevented any of us from seeing and knowing what was going on in the neighborhood. I was sixteen years old when we moved to another more upscale area of the city, so I had already developed what I consider to be my "street smarts".

If there is one thing I remember when I was young is that I never looked down on anybody. Perhaps it's because even as a child there were some people already looking down on me. I instinctively never wanted to make another person feel the same way I did when this happened. There wasn't one person I would ever consider to be less than me or not good enough to be my friend...not even those mischievous neighborhood boys. As I go down memory lane and revisit that very house I grew up in, it no longer holds the negative stigma it once did when I was young. The street is much improved with some houses being torn down and replaced by much nicer ones. It actually looks quite lovely now.

I think one of the best things about being a child is having the innocence to see things in such a lily-white way that we think everyone views the world the same way we do. It's only after we experience the full gamut of life, that we can allow ourselves to openly admit some of our negative experiences. We can become quite jaded if we don't learn from our past. In order to better enjoy our lives, we must make every effort to get past our negative life experiences and learn to look at life from some of our innocent childlike perspective. It's a pretty hard goal to achieve, but I can tell you that it is not impossible. I must admit that it does require a concentrated effort and a lot of work to try to get back some of the little pleasures that we may have enjoyed as children.

"Your living is determined not so much by what life brings to you as by the attitude you bring to life; not so much by what happens to you as by the way your mind looks at what happens." ~ John Homer Miller

It's neat how much information we processed as children and how much we stored in the recesses of our mind. I'm pretty sure you're no different than I am. Parents, whether mine, yours, or your friends are very influential in forming the values, self-image, and self-esteem of young children. Children in their own innocence readily pass along this information. In retrospect when I have a glimpse of it now, I was somehow or other taught to believe that I was less than some of my friends. This is why I came to describe myself as an underdog. It took me a very long time to realize that I was equal to others and that my friends are my peers.

My friend's mother would have been a much kinder person if she took these sage words of advice into consideration... *"As long as you keep a person down, some part of you has to be down there to hold him down, so it means you cannot soar as you otherwise might." ~ Marian Anderson*

Also... *"Never forget that life can only be nobly inspired and rightly lived if you take it bravely and gallantly, as a splendid adventure in which you are setting out into an unknown country, to face many a danger, to meet many a joy, to find many a comrade, to win and lose many a battle." ~ Anne Besant*

Personal Reflections:

1. Have you ever felt as if you were less or not equal to another human being? If so, why?

2. Did another person try to make you feel less than them or look down on someone else in your presence?
3. If so, what did you do about it?

2. Tell another person tonight what you feel love than them or took What an someone take in your presence.

12 ~ Dealing with Depression

"Challenges are what makes life interesting; overcoming them is what makes life meaningful." ~ *Joshua J. Marine*

As expressed earlier, depression is a very complex thing and it has the tendency to touch most of our lives in one way or another. I have read that depression is anger turned in. From my own personal frame of reference, I have come to believe that this can be a true statement depending on an individual's circumstances. Having said that, I have also come to realize that figuring out what we're angry about can be a real challenge.

At times, we become very angry at ourselves and what is going on in our lives. We can also become angry at other people because we may want to blame them for our depressed state or our overall unhappiness. Perhaps our anger is a result of hurt feelings and what other people have said or done to us or what they aren't doing for us. There is a natural tendency to let this anger fester inside so that it becomes so much bigger than it actually is. Our down feelings or depression actually end up feeding, these oftentimes, perceived hurts and resentments.

When we aren't enjoying our lives the way we think we should, we may become frustrated and resentful. We can often think it is someone or something outside of ourselves that is causing us to feel this negative way. Even if the harm that has been done to us is very real, it is very difficult to let go of because it has become such a part of our basic being. In essence, this state of depression or negative life cycle can become like a trusted friend that we rely on as we visit these not so positive feelings over and over again.

It's as if these "down" feelings become comfortable and, at times, we can end up isolating ourselves from other people because they may not feel the same way about our situation as we do. We think that we understand ourselves so much better because we know what has been done to us and what we feel inside. These inner feelings are okay for a time as we work through the healing process and try to better help ourselves but if we stay in this state too long, they can become our true enemy. There is a fine line.

Making the effort to get past the anger in this negative life cycle is a huge decision. It means that we have decided to let go and to move on in a positive direction. It means that we have decided to forgive not only those who have added to our grief, but to also forgive ourselves. It means that we have now taken back the responsibility for the happiness in our own lives. I can assure you that this decision is not for the faint of heart. ***"You must do the thing you think you cannot do." ~ Eleanor Roosevelt***

We must look in the mirror and decide to act. This is a very crucial point in the healing process. It is the very first step in deciding that we truly want a happier self. It's taking back our own personal power. It's realizing that we are accepting the responsibility for the majority of happiness or unhappiness in our own lives by adjusting our own attitude and choices in life. ***"The best thing about the future is that it comes one day at a time." ~ Abraham Lincoln***

There will be steps forward and steps back but in the end if we make up our minds to endure, we will climb this uphill battle and succeed.

I want to stress once again that this is a very crucial decision. It is much more natural to feel like the victim of someone else's bad behavior towards us than it is to grow up and admit that our own slate may not be as sparkly clean as we perceive it to be. It means we must embrace the fact that we may very well have had a hand in what is happening in our lives. It might explain why we lack confidence, self-esteem and may be adding to our own depressed state. Yuck…who really wants to look at themselves in such an analytical way? If we really want to move up the ladder and onto happier times, we must make a momentous decision and take a very big step. This step is what I refer to as the "leap of faith" step because we are also deciding to reach out to a Higher Power and get past these not-so-good feelings about ourselves. You are not alone. Reach down really deep, and there's a hand inside you that will reach back and together you will find the strength, the courage, and the inspiration to move on up so you can better see the light of day.

Winning the battle over depression, will be one of the biggest victories you will ever make in this game called "life".

I know…I've been there.

"Quality is never an accident. It represents the wise choice of many alternatives." ~ Willa Foster

Personal Reflections:
1. Have you ever felt depressed?
2. Do you know what the symptoms of depression entail?
3. Do you believe that you can just "snap out" of a depressed state?
4. If you or someone else you know suffers from depression what is your usual course of action? In

other words, how do you handle it? Do you share your "down" emotional state or do you try to hide it?

13 ~ Life's Journey

"Great minds must be ready not only to take opportunities, but to make them." ~ Colton

Many years ago I decided to take responsibility for the unhappiness in my life and I made several life style changes. One of the biggest and best decisions I ever made was to get on a more regular exercise routine. Although I was fairly young, I never really had much time to dwell on myself because I was busy raising my family and working outside the home as well.

In order to get my life back on track, I decided to begin walking on a regular basis. I started off small by walking in between my bus stop connections on my way home from work instead of merely standing at the bus stop to wait for the next bus. After I built up my stamina and my desire to walk, I would not catch the first bus that came along opting to walk a little farther each day.

Walking brought so much pleasure to my life that I proceeded to increase my distance so that eventually I was able to walk home on some days…a distance of 6 miles. I started this program over twenty-five years ago. I don't think I could even do the math to figure out how many miles I have walked thus far nor calculate the unbelievable benefit I have received from this simple decision so many years ago. I have met several people along the way and enjoyed the company of many other walkers. I still walk three miles every week day and continue to enjoy all the friendships I have made in this special way. At times, it is very difficult to make time for ourselves with the very busy schedules that we all have. However, when we succeed in doing so, in the end everyone benefits. Walking is so simple yet so beneficial. Taking the first step, may very well give you such positive results that you will want to take many more subsequent steps.

Regular exercise of any kind is definitely a good habit and has many other positive side effects. Exercise is very therapeutic in dealing with and managing stress.

"Happiness is not a state to arrive at, but a manner of traveling." ~ Margaret Lee Runbeck

Personal Reflections:

1. Do you endeavor to make time for yourself each day?
2. Do you have a regular exercise routine?
3. Do you sacrifice your own needs in order to meet the needs of others? If you do this, how do you feel about it? When this happens, more often than not, inner

resentment will build up and eventually affect how you view life. In other words, life will seem negative instead of positive.

4. Make time for yourself no matter how busy you are…what can you do to enhance your life as far as exercise is concerned?

14 ~ Dealing with Anger

Every situation properly perceived, becomes an opportunity." ~ Helen Schucman

I have often expressed the view that depression could be a result of anger turned inward. There are many reasons why a person might experience depression but this is merely the one that I am choosing to focus on again in this inspirational book. In my opinion, there is also a genetic predisposition to depression but I won't be discussing that view in this chapter. If interested, I have gone into great depth in one of my other publications **Up The "Down" Ladder** which deals with many of my views on depression as well as some simple ideas to help overcome mild to moderate depression. At times, I have the opportunity to hear the views of others concerning this subject. Some are more willing to share these views than others; however, most prefer to do so based on anonymity. One such comment comes from a personal contact with the pseudonym of Hope. She prefers to remain anonymous and I am honoring her wishes. Her comment inspired me to address the anger issue which most of us face at one time or another in our lives. Being angry is a choice. It is not to say that at times in our lives, we don't have the right to be angry. However, we can choose to admit the emotion we are dealing with and eventually decide to move on to a more positive and upbeat frame of mind. I would like to take this opportunity to share Hope's point of view as she so eloquently speaks on the emotion of anger.

This is the comment almost in its entirety:

"I agree whole wholeheartedly that moving past anger is a decision. Sometimes I think the things that are at the root of our anger are out of our consciousness… I had a very wise person once tell me that when the reason is out of your consciousness, you are still a victim of it. But once you are aware and still acting in the same self-destructive way, you are no longer a victim…you are choosing to be that way and blaming someone else. I think her point was, once you are aware of the self-destructive behavior, then you are wholly responsible for moving on or not. No longer is there room for blame. So that took me a while to digest, but I think now, that it is very true.

It's amazing how powerful you feel, once you realize there is a choice to be angry or not. Simple solution…very difficult to live by. With a daily commitment to think otherwise, there is proportional reprieve of the burden in that day."

I was extremely moved by Hope's insight concerning the subject of anger. I read it over and over again to get the full scope of its meaning. It also made me do more soul-searching and inspired me to write more on the topic of anger. I know a person who has suffered from severe depression for many years. This person has been on a heavy regiment of medication for depression and although it helped somewhat, it never totally eliminated the depressed state.

After many years of suffering, a therapist finally managed to help her get to the bottom of her severe depression. Through counselling and extensive therapy, she was able to finally peel back the layers of what was causing her deep and, often times, debilitating depression. What appeared to be the main cause, although there were other factors, was what she perceived as the consistently bad behavior of her husband throughout their well over thirty years of marriage. After this realization, her depressed state turned outward with the expression of anger toward her husband. Her anger toward him was so great that eventually they had to go their separate ways. Over a span of several years, what was bottled up inside her and coming across as depression was in actuality, extreme anger. In essence, it appeared to be her inability to identify and accept what was really going on in her marriage and effectively deal with it. I don't know if it was a combination of her inadequacy and/or her reluctance to address the real issue but it certainly came back to haunt her marriage. One thing I do know is this...the consequences of her suppressed anger were devastating. This is merely just one case which demonstrates that depression can be a result of anger turned inward. By not facing the reality of her situation sooner, the challenges became too great to overcome and the damage to her marriage was irreversible.

A few years ago in my reading travels I came across these words of wisdom. The source is obscure but the words are well-worth repeating... *"if you are angry, there are three ways you can approach the emotion: express the anger, suppress the anger, calm the anger. Expressing anger in a controlled manner, is a healthy approach. However, this approach is often difficult to do because it involves a balancing act — getting your needs met without hurting others. In short, controlling anger involves respecting both yourself and other people, especially those who are the cause or object of your anger, while still being able to express it. The second approach is suppression. Suppressing anger can backfire. When a person tends to suppress his anger, he can develop high blood pressure, hypertension or even depression. The last approach is calming the anger down. A person who is able to calm his anger down is able to control his outward behavior. However, if he is unable to calm down, he may hurt someone or even himself."*

I very much agree with the author of these words. What is said makes perfect sense to me and perhaps to you too. As you can see it is no easy feat to deal with anger; however, it can have many devastating negative, emotional, and physical consequences if we don't. No matter what…we all experience anger now and then, it is whether we effectively deal with it in a healthy way or not that leads to either a positive or negative result.

"Getting something done is an accomplishment; getting something done right is an achievement." ~ Source Unknown

Personal Reflections

1. Do you agree that we all experience anger at one time or another?
2. Do you consider anger to be a healthy or unhealthy emotion?
3. How are you dealing with your anger? In other words, do you express it or suppress it? Do you feel that you are able to express it in a

controlled manner in order to get your point across or do you "lose it" by engaging in uncontrollable outbursts?

15 ~ Dreams

"Some people dream of worthy accomplishments, while others stay awake and do them." ~ Source Unknown

"To be what we are, and to become what we are capable of becoming, is the only end of life." ~ Robert Louis Stevenson

At times, we don't always realize the importance of our dreams. To me, the ability to dream and to have hope go hand in hand.

To dream is to look ahead and aspire to be more than what we are at the present moment.

To dream is to have the desire to make a difference in this world we call home.

To dream is to be able to look forward and to try to achieve a goal that is new to us or that we thought was unattainable. To accomplish our dream is to realize that our lives are worth living. In doing so we gain self-worth, self-respect, and in most instances the respect of others. This occurs especially when we have gone against the odds and risen above what appears to be the impossible. When we dream, we have hope. When we have hope, we have a reason to live. Our "raison d'être" is the essence of our being. Without it, we don't have much. With it, we have an indomitable spirit that drives us to broaden our horizons and soar with the eagles.

"There is only one thing for us to do, and that is to do our level best right where we are every day of our lives; to use our best judgement, and then to trust the rest to that Power which holds the forces of the universe in His hand..." ~ Orison Swett Marden

"In the moment that you carry this conviction...is that moment your dream will become a reality." ~ Robert Collier

Personal Reflections:

1. The dreams I am referring to in this short chapter are what I consider to be personal aspirations. Do you aspire to be more than you are?
2. Are you able to look down the road at your life and set goals and aspire to accomplish them?
3. Do you give up too soon or do you make every effort to succeed in your personal attempts at greatness?

4. Do you allow the negative opinions of others to deter you in your efforts to pursue your dreams?

16 ~ Childless Mother

Nothing strengthens the judgment and quickens the conscience like individual responsibility." ~ Elizabeth Cady Stanton

Quite a few years back, my husband and I returned from a brief trip to Swift Current to attend our granddaughter's Confirmation. She had chosen her grandpa to be her sponsor. What an incredible honor bestowed upon him. When he received our granddaughter's phone call, I witnessed his pleasure first hand. We hadn't visited with our daughter and her family for several months and we saw a huge change. The girls had grown and matured and as usual we enjoyed our short visit with them.

As was the norm, on our way home in the car we listened to the local radio station to get a bit of news about the surrounding area. The talk show on this particular morning was about an unfortunate car accident that had taken place on March 29, 2009 in a small town just outside of Swift Current.

The topic immediately grabbed our attention because two of the mothers that had lost their daughters in this accident were being interviewed on the car radio about this tragic event. Three young girls, two sixteen years of age as well as a fourteen year old, were making a left turn on the highway when a car driven by a seventeen year old male tried to pass them on the left side. He was driving at 128k/hr. when he collided into their car. All three of the girls died in this horrible car accident. The mothers, the families, and the friends of these young women have been beside themselves with grief over their loss.

The young man happened to be sentenced the week before this radio talk show and the discussion revolved around the punishment he received and whether it was adequate enough. Although the judge gave him a sentence to suit his age when the accident occurred, by the time of the trial he was eighteen years old. Some people called in to express their opinion by stating that he did not receive a long enough sentence for the crime committed.

My heart goes out to the mothers who lost their daughters in the prime of their lives and in such a tragic way. Both of the mothers being interviewed were compassionate and open-minded despite their unbelievable loss. However, comments were made by some callers citing that this young man had his whole life to live while the girls had so sadly lost theirs by his reckless actions. Others felt that he did not show enough remorse.

Later on in the talk show, I briefly heard a comment from another caller who probably knew the boy's family. She stated that the young man was struggling with his life. My heart immediately went out to him and his mother as well. Unless this man has no conscience at all, I cannot fathom that he has been unaffected by having had a hand in the death of these three young women.

I would have to think that he will somehow or other be scarred for life. He lives in a small town where he will have little or no anonymity. He will live with the reality of his careless actions for the rest of his life. He will probably marry one day and have children of his own. He may very well learn to pray and appreciate the quality of life when he faces his actions as a more mature individual.

Yes, those young girls, their families, and their friends got robbed; however, I personally do not envy the life that this young man now has to live. Anyone who thinks it is going to be easy is only fooling him/herself. I also feel a sense of compassion for this young man, his family, and his friends. I'm sure his mother's heart is aching because there is much more to face in her son's life and he will need the support of them all.

They all lost so much that fateful day and their lives are forever changed. Three mothers lost the lives of their daughters on March 29, 2009 and one mother lost the innocence that her young son can no longer enjoy. All four mothers lost children that tragic day. Only now, one will be haunted by his reckless actions for the rest of his life.

"There are many truths of which the full meaning cannot be realized until personal experience has brought it home." ~ John Stuart Mill

Personal Reflections:
1. Have you experienced personal loss whereby you hold another person responsible for that loss?
2. Is it an easy feat to forgive someone who has so carelessly taken from you?
3. What are the consequences if you don't? In other words, who are you hurting if you harbor anger and resentment?
4. Give yourself the time to heal but in the end the best remedy is to "let go, let God". Do you think that by tapping into your faith, you will be more able to forgive the offender?

17 ~ Having a Bad Day

"Take each day and relish each moment. Take each bad day and work to make it good." ~ Lisa Dado

"If you get a second chance, grab it with both hands. If it changes your life, let it. Nobody said life would be easy, they just promised it would be worth it." ~ Source Unknown

I want to share a cute little story with you to demonstrate how simple it is to turn your life around one step at a time. Many years ago when I was working downtown in a major mall, oftentimes, I would go shopping during my lunch hour. This mall consisted of many businesses, retail stores, restaurants, and pretty well everything working people might want at their fingertips.

On this particular day, I was having one of my "off" days. We all have these kinds of days now and then, but this one was particularly bad. As mentioned in some of my earlier chapters, I suffer from depression and I could sense that I was headed in that direction if I didn't take positive action. I decided I would go for a walk in the mall because I wasn't what one might consider to be "good company" in this rather foul mood of mine.

As I was walking along, I was wondering what I could do to cheer myself up and make for a better day. When I finally reached a section of the mall that had an outside door, I noticed a somewhat bedraggled man sifting through the sand in one of the big ashtrays near the entrance to the mall. There was no smoking allowed in this huge underground facility so anyone that came through the door had to "butt out".

It was obvious to me that this poor man was searching for the longest butts in the ashtray so he could have a few good puffs. By the way he was dressed and by his actions, it was apparent to me that he could not afford to buy his own cigarettes. Just looking at him and what he was doing made me forget all about my woes and my bad day.

As I focused on him a light bulb went on in my head and I decided to do a good deed or a random act of kindness. Over twenty years ago, to my knowledge no one referred to these acts by that term, but it doesn't mean to say that they weren't happening just the same. I went up to this man and gently asked him to wait right where he was standing. He looked up at me and nodded his head in agreement.

I turned around and went into a nearby drugstore and bought a large package of cigarettes and some matches. This was a time when smoking wasn't as nearly frowned upon as it is today. After purchasing the cigarettes, I quickly walked back to where the man was standing and handed him my recent purchase, receipt and all. I didn't want anyone to think he had stolen the cigarettes should he be seen with them. I suggested that he enjoy his gift and perhaps share them with some of his friends. He was very pleased, but what he said after that, changed my mood for the whole day and many days afterward.

This was a Monday, and Mondays can be kind of blue at times, just as it was for me that particular day. When this less fortunate man thanked me for the cigarettes, he quickly added, "What are you doing next Monday?" I almost laughed out loud because I found his question so surprising and somewhat amusing. He completely caught me off guard. He was planning on meeting me there as often as possible, perhaps every Monday if I was willing. It was such a cute response. I couldn't help but smile at him as I told him that this was just a spontaneous, one time occurrence and I just wanted to make his day.

In essence the exact opposite happened, he made mine instead. By reaching out to someone with a greater need than my own and giving in such a small way, it made me realize that it truly is better to give than to receive. I was given so much that precious day because even after all these years, the memory of that incident still brings a smile to my face. By doing what I did, I discovered that *"no one is in charge of your happiness but you". ~ Regina Brett*

This little story reminded me of how fortunate I really was and how by going out of my way to make a less fortunate person have a good day, it actually ended up creating a better one for me. You really cannot give away a kindness in life.

The pleasure that this man had on his face was a hugely rewarding experience. He was very grateful and he thanked me for my kindness. However, it was me who had every reason to thank him for accepting my simple gift and getting me out of my funk. He was the one being kind and gracious. He did not get offended by my gesture. He made me smile and managed to elevate my mood by showing his gratefulness that blue Monday so many years ago.

"You may be dead broke and that's a reality, but in spirit you may be brimming over with optimism, joy, and energy. The reality of your life may result from many outside factors, none of which you have control. Your attitudes, however, reflect the ways in which you evaluate what is happening." ~ H. Stanley Judd

Personal Reflections:

1. Do you ever have bad days?
2. If so, what do you usually do about it?
3. Have you created simple, little ways to help get yourself out of your "funks" before a deeper depression sets in?
4. Do you engage in random acts of kindness?

18 ~ Forgiveness

Be kind and compassionate to one another, forgiving each other, just as in Christ God forgave you." ~ Ephesians 4:32

I love this biblical quote. It demonstrates to me that I am to forgive others "just as" Christ has forgiven me. Perhaps, I see things a little differently than some other people when it comes to forgiveness but I would like to take this opportunity to explain my views. I know it has been said that we will not be forgiven "until" or "unless" we forgive others. However, according to the above biblical quote, I believe that I can also go to God as a sinner and seek forgiveness for myself from Him. When I experience His generous gift of forgiveness and mercy, I then learn to forgive others in the same way that I have been forgiven. In other words, I am emulating God's forgiveness, "just as Christ God forgave" me.

I believe God set the ultimate example of forgiveness by dying on the cross for my sins and I have the option of going humbly before Him and accepting His forgiveness. He's the ultimate Teacher, not me. I personally need to learn from the Master. It's not me showing God how I forgave so that I may be forgiven, but rather, it is God showing me how to forgive by first forgiving me for my sins and indiscretions so that I can go on to forgive others who have wronged me.

In my situation and perhaps in other's as well, by following His holy actions I am better equipped to forgive others because I have learned from the greatest Forgiver of all times. When we accept Jesus as our personal Savior, we not only want to forgive, it becomes a way of life as we follow in Jesus' footsteps and forgive others as we have been forgiven by God Himself. In essence, I have chosen to first look at my own sinfulness, human weaknesses, and need for forgiveness. I have made a conscious choice to do this instead of looking at how others have wronged me and my need to forgive them in order to be forgiven by Christ. Once I see my own weaknesses and ask for God's forgiveness, I am better able to accept the weaknesses of others and forgive them theirs. The above biblical quote as well as the following one helped inspire my interpretation on forgiveness…forgive each other "as the Lord has forgiven you".

"Bearing with one another and, if one has a complaint against another, forgiving each other; as the Lord has forgiven you, so you also must forgive."
~ Colossians 3:13

This third biblical quote by Matthew says it a little differently...more like the "until" or "unless" or "if" description of forgiveness that some other people might use to describe what a sinner must do to be forgiven.

"For if you forgive men when they sin against you, your heavenly Father will also forgive you." ~ Matthew 6:14

Perhaps, either way we choose to look at the power of forgiveness, whether we repent and seek it, or whether we forgive others then seek it...if we end up at the foot of the Cross, we are ultimately forgiven our transgressions. I don't think the act of forgiveness is about drawing a line in the sand or an "either/or" type of concept. It's not about if you don't do things the way I think they should be done, then it's the wrong way. It's also not about trying to force people to think like we do or by expressing that somehow or other we are closer to God than they are. Our relationships with God are very personal because we are all unique individuals. With that in mind, it is wise to acknowledge that each relationship with God is as unique as our personalities. Therefore, it is necessary to respect each other and trust that God has a plan for each of us even if it is a bit different from someone else's path. Our heavenly Father has taken our uniqueness into consideration when forming our relationship with Him and He knows exactly how to draw us closer to Him. For that, I am eternally grateful!

Personal Reflections:

1. Do you know anyone who tries to get you to share their religious views?
2. How do you view this behavior?
3. Do you engage in this type of behavior yourself…that of trying to get others to think like you?
4. Have you considered that actions speak louder than words?
5. The best way to get people to believe in Christ is to set the example so that people will want to emulate you. Do you agree?

19 ~ Added Talent

The following four stories have been penned by my sisters at my personal request. They have generously agreed to share their talent with my reading audience and I am delighted. The first story is written by my oldest sister, Shirley Gauthier Sarafinchan who has also agreed to let me use some of her many beautiful pictures for the covers of my books. I am publishing each of their stories according to their birth order in our family to demonstrate a sense of fairness and equality amongst us as a family. Linda Briscoe is the third daughter after me with Lorraine Gauthier and Gloria Korell being the youngest girls in the family. We also have a brother, Ron Gauthier, who is the eldest adult child and only son. I enjoyed each of the stories provided by my sisters as they reflected on cherished moments in their lives. I thought, you as my readers, would enjoy them as well. Thank you to my sisters and also to each of you for honoring us by reading this inspirational book.

The Old Farmhouse
Shirley Gauthier Sarafinchan

This poem was originally written on April 30th, 1981 about an old farmhouse that was once home to a family but sometime later I associated it with abused women. In essence, it reminded me of women who strive so very hard to make homes for their families. No matter how hard they try, they are worn down and battered. Finally they have the opportunity and the strength to stand up for their rights and to free themselves from their bondage to at last find the peace and solace that they so richly deserve. The old farmhouse is a symbol of a refuge for abused women.

THE OLD FARMHOUSE

Amid the fields it stands so alone, so serene, so peaceful, yet filled with an emptiness all its own, this old farmhouse that was once called home.

Its shingles torn and tattered, windows scarce of glass, doors hanging by a single hinge alas this old farmhouse so battered.

What secrets dare to lie within its walls, love, laughter, fun and joy, echoes of little children running down the halls, tears, sorrow and pain for loved ones lost?

Music must have filled the nights with sounds of crickets and birds in flight, the sweet scent of the prairie harvest and wild flowers a pleasant sight.

The tantalizing aroma of freshly baked bread reaching every corner of the old farmhouse and early morning sunrises filling each room full of light, the warmth from the wood stove soon to spread.

Memories fill this old farmhouse, nothing more is really left but, it has served its purpose in this life and now alone, it can be at rest.

Remembering When
Linda Briscoe

When I was a child we walked to school on the very first day! Brand new outfit and school bag, packed with crayons and all new supplies. I walked and walked for what seemed like forever, happy to finally be at school, only to realize that there would be the same walk home at lunch, then back to school and home again!

The days would be glorious in the fall, still warm enough for just a sweater. The leaves would start to fall to the ground and the winds would pick up. Before I knew it, the cold would be in the not too distant future. It was time to bundle up to make the walk to school as bearable as possible. Now, in the bitterness of winter, lunch bag packed, off to school I went. Bundled tightly, with my scarf around my forehead and neck, I braved the long walk to school. Oh…it could get bitterly cold, so cold as the wind blew through my not so warm coat and the well-worn boots which had known other winters. Is this cold winter ever going to pass?

Then it changed. The days started getting longer, the sun started getting stronger, and I was very excited as I could spot the first patch of pavement. The ditches were so inviting filled with melting ice and water. Trusting to step on the now thin ice and not sink…only to find a boot full of water was merely a fine line away…just one more step and a little more pressure before the ice cracked and I could feel the SPLOOSH as the cold water seeped into my boots. A young child and a ditch full of water are like two magnets being drawn to each other.

On that walk home from school, the snow was only going to bring the worst of spring, with its dirty snow banks and slippery sidewalks after a cold night. Getting splashed by a passing car was the norm as I surged forward on my long walk home. Try as I might to keep my spring coat clean and the runners that I changed into after school as I rid myself of my heavy rubber boots was an impossible feat.

Through the Eyes of a Child
Lorraine Gauthier

As children, with the purest of hearts we see life with wonder. We learn to walk by crawling, standing, and falling…so similar to life as an adult. We educate ourselves by seeing, hearing and copying those we want to be like…a parent, an older sibling, or a friend.

We all started off as children and somewhere in us, we still have the heart of that young child. I know I still do. As an innocent child, I usually chose to do things for the absolute right reason. At age two, I chose to cut off my hair to look like a boy. The reason…my dad had 'hoped' I was a boy because he wanted another son after my brother and three sisters were born. I loved him and wanted to please him. I wanted to give him what I 'thought' was a boy, as if cutting off my hair would do the trick.

Years later, we had another girl born into our family. Now there were five girls. We had a small house and had to learn how to share. We were lucky to get a new chest of drawers. This was very exciting to me because now we could each have our own drawer for our personal belongings. However, I was worried that we, as sisters, wouldn't recognize our own drawer. I decided to engrave our names on each drawer so that my sisters knew which one was theirs. Needless to say, this was not well received. My dad was furious. I was punished because I had damaged the new chest of drawers

How many times in life, even as an adult, do we have perfectly good intentions, with the purest of hearts, yet it is received differently? I am grateful that throughout our lives we can still have the heart of a child. Over the years, this child's heart will feel both joy and pain. It truly becomes our guide to how we perceive things as an adult. Hopefully, we can continue to see the beauty in all things like we did as an innocent child!

Siloam Mission
Gloria Korell

In the past few months I had the privilege of volunteering at Siloam Mission with my daughter Meagan. I experienced firsthand what it was like to do "God's work". Observing the volunteers, people of all races and ages, working in such harmony to provide for the patrons of Siloam gave me the impression the work was effortless. The eagerness to prepare a meal and clean up afterwards with such smiling faces and cheery hearts delivered a strong message about the rewards of giving.

My first visit to Siloam left me with a different opinion of the homeless. I discovered that they could be one of us and we could be one of them and as my volunteer experience continued so did my connection with these people. We so often take for granted our blessings in life. In the weeks following, each time I visited Siloam the rewards became greater. In a strange way I was becoming "addicted". I needed to feel the "high" from giving. It felt like I was becoming needy myself. I wanted to continually hand over that plate of food so I could hear the thank you or see a smile on someone's face.

Yes, the significance of people needing one another. My need was just as great as theirs. As a result, this experience has been one of the most rewarding in my life and I am grateful my daughter had the opportunity to open her heart and give to others less fortunate. All our experiences in life help us to "connect the dots" on our journey. For me, this experience not only opened my eyes, but also my heart and it made me realize that I too was being fed.

CONCLUSION
~ New Endings~

How many times in life do we live with regrets? We look back and sometimes our lives haven't gone quite the way we hoped for or expected. We get so disappointed and discouraged with ourselves, our lives, and with the people around us. No one can change the past, not even God. What's done is done. The key to living a peaceful life is to not let the past affect our present or future happiness.

There's nothing wrong with looking back and learning from our past mistakes but rather than mourn the loss of what could have been, we can choose to start now to make a new ending. By doing so, we can change the outcome of future events. Our lives can hold a much brighter future when we look ahead with faith and courage.

Faith in God and a renewed faith in ourselves…because we have taken the time to look in the mirror and realize as well as capitalize on the personal power that we possess in order to start now and create a new, more positive, and acceptable ending to our lives. Go for it!

Life is too short to wake up with regrets. So love the people who treat you right. Forget the ones who don't.

believe everything happens for a reason, a season, or a lifetime.

Bonus Chapter

A Woman's Voice ~ Volume 1
1 ~ The Empty Nest

The house is quiet as we both go about our usual business. We are never alone despite the silence that endures between us. This is a result of a true and unending love relationship that started as a friendship between my husband and me.

After over forty years of marriage, sharing a home, first only with each other...then raising a family, we sit in the peaceful silence of our empty nest knowing that this is our quiet time together. We have not entered our twilight years lightly nor without great thought and careful planning. We know that we are on the home stretch of, not only our years together, but of our very lives. We have more years to look back on than ahead. It is good...in fact, it is more than good, it is all that I could have ever dreamed of or hoped for in the life that has been given to me. I am forever grateful to have been given so much. I take nothing for granted and each day I thank God for my many blessings.

Some refer to this stage of life as the "empty nest" while I prefer to see it as the stage of life when we can sit back and be grateful for having survived its challenges. It is not an easy feat to simultaneously marry young, educate ourselves, and raise a family. We all go through the growing pains that must take place in order to accomplish and succeed in our efforts to have a successful marriage. Yet, I'm not so sure what appears to be a successful marriage is always a happy one…by that, I mean would you do it all over again if the choice was yours to make?

At this moment in time, I find myself more content and reflective. I not only have embraced this quiet time of my life, I have worked toward it. This opportunity leads to numerous seeds ready to germinate into the little stories I so deeply enjoy sharing. Not too long ago, one of my fellow authors suggested it would be a great book idea to write about the ingredients that make up a really good marriage, not a marriage that one endures but rather a holy union that one would eagerly say "yes" to again if they had to start all over.

Take a moment to just sit there and reflect. Think about the person you are married to and how you view him/her. Just between you and your Maker, would you honestly marry this person again? Be really honest now? Remember, if you can't be honest in this personal quiet time when you look at your spouse, it will be very difficult for you to be honest in your relationship. So….would you actually marry your spouse knowing all that you do today? I'm just asking for a simple 'yes or no'. No more, no less. I don't want to hear a maybe because it implies that you want your spouse to change. That's not what this is all about. Plain and simple…would you marry your spouse again if given a second chance to choose otherwise?

If the answer is a resounding no, then my next question is why? Is your spouse such a disappointment to you that if given a second chance you might say 'no' or 'maybe if'? Is it really about misplaced expectations or is it about not knowing what true love really is? A relative once stated that I had a perfect marriage. I would have to disagree. To have a perfect marriage implies perfection or a union of two perfect people. Most of us know full well that such a concept is absolutely impossible and does not exist, at least not on this side of the turf…but I do believe in perfect love. To me, perfect love is learning to love and accept your spouse no matter what. All you need to do is refer to those old-fashioned marriage vows to get my drift. Do you still believe in those words…if so, you are on the right track? All you need to do is visualize yourself riding off into the sunset with your better half.

If you can do this…the sky's the limit.

"Love means the body, the soul, the life, the entire being. We feel love as we feel the warmth of our blood, we breathe love as we breathe the air, we hold it in ourselves as we hold our thoughts. Nothing more exists for us." ~ Guy De Maupassant

"How you react towards your spouse is a choice rooted in your heart." ~ Jim Hughes

BONUS CHAPTERS
Growing Up and Liking It ~ More Steps To A Happier Self ~
Introduction

I am back to write the second half of my suggestions for a happier self. The first half found in *I'm Not Perfect And It's Okay* consisted of thirteen steps. I considered this to be the bulk of my suggestions. The tips in this book are what I am going to refer to as the "donut holes," and they will finish off the theme of the first book. At this point, I think that these chapters will be shorter, not unlike the center of the donuts being smaller than the donut itself, but tasty just the same. Hopefully, these will be just as good as the original baker's dozen and, although not as long, equally easy to comprehend and digest.

Once again, I must admit that I never considered myself to be an author when I first started to put pen to paper. My need to write far outweighed my literary expertise. I will also admit that as time goes by, I see myself as much more of a philosopher than an author in the sense that I do a lot of thinking and analyzing before I attempt to write anything down. I have been mulling over these thoughts, not only for a number of months, but literally for a number of years. As the years go by, however, my passion for writing and the desire for my voice to be heard increases. Perhaps like the honing of any other skill, I now classify myself as a motivational author. My writing is meant for others who think like me or who can relate to some of the experiences I am about to share with you. Plain and simple, this is what I consider to be a heart book. It's written from my heart to any and all hearts that are open to its message.

My previous book has been a series of essays that have brought me great joy in the writing of them. I agree with Charles Poore in saying that, "An essayist is a lucky person who has found a way to discourse without being interrupted."[1] I believe I am one of these lucky people who have been given both the inspiration and the opportunity. If you have not read my first book, I would encourage you to do so. If you already have and are reading this book, I thank you from the bottom of my heart for allowing me to share my "bits of wisdom" with you yet again.

Many times in life people offer advice without the benefit of the voice of experience. The suggestions that I offered in my first book as well as the tips I am about to offer in *Growing Up and Liking It* are based on personal experience. I know that they work because I have lived them. When I struggle in life, it is most often as a result of losing sight of my own recommendations. It is at this time that I find it necessary to remind myself of the steps I have suggested for the benefit of all, including myself. When this occurs, I usually do a reality check to ensure that I am practicing what I teach. I have chosen to use the word *teach* instead of *preach* out of personal preference for "it's easier to preach ten sermons than it is to live one."[2] If and when you really want to improve your life, the steps provided are a sure proof method to a more enjoyable life. These steps are not about removing your woes but rather about providing ideas for a better coping mechanism that may improve your ability to face what life has to offer. Always try to remember that "the Will of God will never take you where the Grace of God will not protect you."[3] I have really learned to grow up over the last several years, and it has been beneficial to all, especially me and those closest to me. This is the reason why I think the title to my book is so appropriate. As I enter into my twilight years, I want to permanently shed my insecurities and enter this final stage of life with as much grace and wisdom as humanly possible. I have been an observant student for the majority of my life. Perhaps now, after all these years, I can get into the driver's seat and call myself a good teacher. I have succeeded in learning to "teach without classroom walls" and I have now written my own motivational books to go along with this philosophy. This experience has been extremely liberating for me. I hope by reading what I have to say and by incorporating some of my suggestions into your life, that you too can find a sense of true freedom and peace.

Shake It Off

What better way to start off this book than with the telling of a story? Some things never change! The story I am about to tell you is actually one of the reasons I am writing this second book. After writing thirteen chapters, I wasn't sure if I had thirteen more points to offer. I knew that I had more to say/write, so I'm starting off not knowing just how far this book will go. I am optimistic nonetheless because once I started to write my first book I never ceased to amaze even myself as the ideas continued to flow one after the other. Once again, I cannot take full credit for these ideas as I remind myself that, at times, they seem to come to me from a well much deeper than my own. In advance, I already know that I will be drawing from this same resource. This was the inspiration for my first book, which was based on my own, personal relationship with God. I am forever grateful for this "gift" of insight, which has been bestowed upon me and many others before me. I have learned that "the task ahead of us is never as great as the power behind us."[4] This has been demonstrated by the wealth of quotes, bits of expertise, and words of wisdom that I have been able to share with you as I tell my story. "Honesty is the first chapter in the book of wisdom."[5] Due to the fact that honesty is one of the characteristics that I most highly regard, I have made every effort to relate all my stories as honestly and as accurately as possible. I know that honesty and wisdom go hand and hand. Wisdom is another trait I hold in high esteem, and I will continue to incorporate the "little bits" of it that I have observed or used along the way as I share my ideas with you.

Several years ago when my husband was enjoying a hockey game at our local arena, not unlike many of the other spectators at the event, he needed a washroom break. I don't know if your arena is like ours, but most sport venues never seem to have enough bathrooms. There are always long lines. It isn't so bad if you use the facilities during the game; however, if you need to use them during intermission, you can be sure that the people will be lined up. Sometimes the queue is right out the door. Obviously, because this event occurred in the male washroom, I am only repeating this story as told to me by my husband when he got home from the hockey game. He still had laughter in his voice as he tried to describe it to me.

Often times, you can try to retell a story but for some reason or another, it doesn't always have the same funny effect. I must say that this was the exception because I found this story every bit as cute and as funny as my husband did. As he was waiting in line, he noticed a father in the washroom with his young son. The father was trying to force the boy to hurry up as he was using the facilities due to the long line up of other men waiting for their turns. The young boy just looked up at his dad and said that he wasn't finished. He added that he needed time to "shake it off." My husband went on to say that the whole room cracked up with laughter over what the little boy had said because all of them could relate to it. That little boy wasn't going anywhere until he had finished what he had started. He was taking care of business in the way that his father had taught him on many earlier occasions. It was the only way he knew how to do what he needed to get done. "In every child who is born, under no matter what circumstances, and of no matter what parents, the potentiality of the human race is born again."[6] So simple was this basic act, taught to this young boy, at such an early stage of life.

How powerful our role is as parents and educators. No matter how many other men were in the room, that young son knew that his dad had taught him how to do things right. Therefore, it was exactly what he intended to do. He had no idea what everyone found so amusing. He was only finishing what he had started because he had complete and total trust in what his dad had taught him. There was no question about it! In fact, he had so much faith in what his father had taught him that he took the opportunity to remind him of it. "Small opportunities are often the beginning of great enterprises."[7] The lessons were twofold in the sense that the lad was doing as he had been instructed, and the dad was learning just how powerful he was in the teaching of one of life's simple lessons. These simple, little everyday lessons are the first stepping stones for all the lessons to follow. That young boy, at least at this impressionable age, was learning to emulate his father in all that he did or had been taught to do. Yes, he wasn't quite finished yet.

Therefore, I too must learn from one of my life lessons. Although these chapters may be shorter, I still must finish what I started. I feel it is necessary to write this second one in order to tie up the loose ends after the first book. For all I know, there could even be a third! It is the only way that I know how to get the job done.

My daughter, who had first shown an interest in my notebook of special quotes and notes, amused me the other day when she agreed that she couldn't see a book in them. She made me chuckle when she said, "It really was about reading between the lines." How true! I've noticed that since my husband has also read my book, I'm starting to hear more and more of my own philosophy on life with the odd quote thrown in. I'm starting to wonder if this is my biggest dream come true or my worst nightmare. We really are on a level playing field. My family now has access to all my little quotes and quips right at their fingertips ready to regurgitate them as the need arises. They now know me inside and out, and my life is fast becoming like an open book. Not to worry, however, because I have been enjoying this information for years. No sooner will they make use of one of my famous quotes when dealing with me, I will come up with a new one, not unlike the missing baby tooth that has been replaced by a permanent one. Such fun, this verbal sparring has become. It really does keep one mentally alert! "The quality of a person's life is in direct proportion to their commitment to excellence, regardless of their chosen field of endeavour."[8] So once again, I stress that it is not so much about what you do but more about how you do it that counts. This could get both interesting and challenging as I try to keep one step ahead of the game as I finish what I have started. It seems that I am sticking my neck even farther out on a limb with my views but I believe it is a risk worth taking.

In most instances, discussing our views and opinions is a good thing. I agree with Bernard Edmonds when he says, "To dream anything that you want to dream, that is the beauty of the human mind. To do anything that you want to do, that is the strength of the human will. To trust yourself to test your limits, that is the courage to succeed."[9] With that thought in mind, I have now completed the essence of the first chapter of my second book. I have every intention of finishing what I have started as I search for the excellence that I feel we are all capable of, no matter what our walk in life may be, as long as we have the desire to succeed. "The difference between a successful person and others is not a lack of strength, not a lack of knowledge, but rather a lack of will."[10] Not unlike that little boy, I too have been taught to finish the job. I have both the desire and the need to do it right, even if it is only according to my own experiences and expectations of myself. Once again, my desire is to share what those experiences have taught me along the way. Some of these findings may also be of benefit to you. I sincerely hope so!

Step 1 ~ It does not matter when you started a special project or had a big dream. What matters is being open to fulfilling that dream when the time is right. Don't stop until you have had the opportunity to "shake it off." When the job is complete, you'll know. It's a great idea to set aside some personal time as often as possible to do a little soul searching in order to fully benefit from all my suggestions. These are just a few examples of some questions that you can ask yourself to better implement the first step. What goals have you set for yourself? Have you written them down?

Create a dream board and clip out pictures or quotes that remind you of your goals every day. Place your board in an area where you'll see it and be inspired by it daily.

ENDNOTES

[1] "Charles Poore quotes," Thinkexist.com, http://thinkexist.com/quotes/charles_poore/.
[2] "Author Unknown," Religious One Liners, http://www.joe-ks.com/archives_feb2007/Religious_One_Liners.htm.
[3] "Author Unknown," Talk Jesus, http://www.talkjesus.com/lounge/6828-will-god-will-never-take-you.html.
[4] "Ralph Waldo Emerson quotes," About.com:Quotations, http://quotations.about.com/od/stillmorefamouspeople/a/Ralph Waldo Emerson.htm.
[5] "Thomas Jefferson quotes," Quoteworld.org, http://www.quoteworld.org/quotes/7147.
[6] "James Agee quotes," Quoteworld.org, http://www.quoteworld.org/quotes/233.
[7] "Demosthenes quotes," The Quotation Page, http://www.quotationspage.com/quote/29680.html.
[8] "Vincent T. Lombardi quotes," Quoteworld.org, http://www.quoteworld.org/quotes/8402.
[9] "Bernard Edmond quotes," Quoteworld.org, http://www.quoteworld.org/quotes/4004.
[10] "Vincent T. Lombardi quotes," Quoteworld.org, http://www.quoteworld.org/quotes/8403.

TO CONTACT AUTHOR:

WEBSITE

http://www.doloresayotte.com

BLOG SITE

http://www.doloresayotte.wordpress.com

FACEBOOK AUTHOR'S PAGE

http://www.facebook.com/Author.Dolores.Ayotte

www.ingramcontent.com/pod-product-compliance
Lightning Source LLC
Chambersburg PA
CBHW071309060426
42444CB00034B/1741